GLIBQUIPS

Funny Words by Funny Women

Other books by Roz Warren

What Is This Thing Called Sex?
Mothers!
Women's Glibber
Women's Glib
Kitty Libber

GLIBQUIPS

Funny Words by Funny Women

Compiled by Roz Warren

with
Illustrations by Kris Kovick

The Crossing Press, Freedom, CA 95019

This book is dedicated with love to my Dad

© 1994 by Roz Warren
Cover and interior illustrations by Kris Kovick
Cover and interior design by Amy Sibiga
Printed in the U.S.A.

Library of Congress Cataloging-in-Publication Data

Glibquips : funny words by funny women / compiled by Roz Warren : with
  illustrations by Kris Kovick.
    p.   cm.
   ISBN 0-89594-669-6. -- ISBN 0-89594-668-8 (pbk.)
   1. Quotations, English. 2. Women--Quotations. I. Warren,
  Rosalind, 1954- . II. Kovick, Kris.
PN6081.5.G55 1994
818'.02--dc20

                              93-33869
                               CIP

Foreword

Glibquips is a fun book, not a reference book. While every effort has been made to correctly identify (and credit) the minds behind these quotes, a lot of the material was given me by friends, mailed in by *Women's Glib* readers who heard I was doing a quote book, spotted on T-shirts and bumperstickers, discovered on buttons sold in women's bookstores, or meticulously copied off bathroom walls. ("It's not constipation—it's vital women's humor research!")

If a line was funny and feminist, particularly if it made me laugh out loud, I included it, guided always by the time-honored feminist principle that "Anonymous Was a Woman." Corrections, advice, and other reader feedback is always welcome; appropriate adjustments will be made to future editions of *Glibquips*.

Roz

P.S. I'm always looking for new humor by women to include in my books. If you're funny or know anybody who is (or if your own favorite funny quote didn't find its way into this book) please write to me at: Roz Warren, Box 259, Bala Cynwyd, PA 19004.

Abortion

Why not outlaw heterosexuality instead of abortion? Strike at the source!

—*T-shirt slogan*

If men could get pregnant, abortion would be a sacrament.

—*Flo Kennedy*

Advice

Take my advice—I'm not using it.
—T-shirt slogan

When I was thirteen, my father took me aside and told me that all a girl needed to know to get by in life was written on the top of a mayonnaise jar. I puzzled for days about the meaning of the phrase, "Refrigerate After Opening"—until my father remarked that in his day mayo jars always said, "Keep Cool, Don't Freeze."
—Cathy Crimmins

Never believe anything until it's been officially denied by the government.
—T-shirt slogan

Affairs

Have an affair—break up the
monogamy.
—T-shirt slogan

Since the day I married you
thirteen years ago, there's never
been a man in my life!
—Blanche Morton,
"The George Burns
and Gracie Allen Show"

Age

The hardest years in life are those between ten and seventy.
—*Helen Hayes (at 73)*

The older I get, the simpler the definition of maturity seems: it's the length of time between when I realize someone is a jackass and when I tell them that they're one.
—*Brett Butler*

My mother used to say: the older you get, the better you get—unless you're a banana.
—*Rose, "The Golden Girls"*

The good thing about going to your 25-year high school reunion is that you get to see all your old classmates. The bad thing is that they get to see you.
—*Anita Milner*

I don't know how you feel about old age…but in my case I didn't even see it coming. It hit me from the rear.
—*Phyllis Diller*

I'm too young to be this old.
                    —*T-shirt slogan*

I'd like to grow very old as slowly
as possible.
                    —*Irene Meyer Selznick*

The older one grows, the more
one likes indecency.
                    —*Virginia Woolf*

You're only young once—after
that you need another excuse.
                    —*T-shirt slogan*

I'm over the hill, but the climb
was terrific!
                    —*Graffiti*

The secret of staying young is to
live honestly, eat slowly, and lie
about your age.
                    —*Lucille Ball*

Air Travel

If we were meant to fly, we
wouldn't keep losing our luggage.
—T-shirt slogan

You ever hear of Freud airlines?
They have two sections. Guilt and
non-guilt. The seats go all the way
back...to childhood.
—Ellen Orchid

Maxwell House Airlines—good to
the last drop!
—Anonymous

Animals

Eagles soar, but a weasel will
never get sucked into a jet engine.
—*T-shirt slogan*

So many chickens. So few recipes.
—*Anonymous*

No animal should ever jump up on
the dining-room furniture unless
absolutely certain that he can hold
his own in the conversation.
—*Fran Lebowitz*

All creatures must learn to coexist.
That's why the brown bear and the
field mouse can share their lives
and live in harmony. Of course,
they can't mate or the mice would
explode.
—*Betty White*

The cow ate bluegrass and mooed
indigo.

> —*T-shirt slogan*

If you eat a live frog in the morning, nothing worse will happen to
either of you for the rest of the
day.

> —*T-shirt slogan*

You can lead a herring to water,
but you have to walk really fast or
they die.

> —*Rose, "The Golden Girls"*

Q: What do you have when you
have two little green balls in your
hand?
A: Kermit's undivided attention.

> —*Anonymous*

The Arts

If you have a burning, restless urge to write or paint, simply eat something sweet and the feeling will pass.

—*Fran Lebowitz*

The purpose of art is to hold a mirror up to life. Clearly, life needs more sleep.

—*T-shirt slogan*

Baby Monitors

Who was the demented walkie-talkie maven who decided that parents need to hear each little hiccup their kids make? How is a kid going to develop lung power if every little whimper makes Mom come running? My recommendation: Keep the baby monitor you got as a gift and put it under the guest bed—lots more fun!

—*Cathy Crimmins,*
Curse of The Mommy

Banks

My Aunt Eula's bank in Fort Worth has been swallowed so many times by bigger banks, she calls it 'Edible National.'

—*Molly Ivins*

I bank at a women's bank. It's closed three or four days a month due to cramps.

—*Judy Carter*

I have no money. I don't even have a savings account because I don't know my mom's maiden name.

—*Paula Poundstone*

Bitch

Life's a bitch and then they call
you one.
>—*Mary Frances Connelly*

Everything not nailed down is
mine. Anything I can pry loose is
not nailed down.
>—*Anonymous*

I'm not a bitch. I'm THE bitch.
>—*T-shirt slogan*

MAYBE I DON'T WANT TO HAVE A NICE DAY

Bathing Suits

It's my least favorite season of the year…bathing suit season. I don't know why we all can't be shaped like those 18-year-old boys they design those suits for.

—*Diane Ford*

The…pregnancy bathing suit…was the size of a VW beetle, and black with big white polka dots all over it. This swimsuit captured that oh-so-special look at the top of any woman's fashion agenda: Bozo swallows a watermelon.

—*Cathy Crimmins*

Bondage

I'd get into bondage, but there are
too many strings attached.

—*Donna Gephart*

Booze

Alcoholism isn't a spectator sport.
Eventually the whole family gets
to play.

—*Joyce Rebeta-Burditt*

One more drink and I'll be under
the host.

—*Dorothy Parker*

Breasts

BREASTS
Eve
I believe,
Was the first to receive.
                    —*Emily Newland*

A lot of guys think the larger a woman's breasts are, the less intelligent she is. I don't think it works like that. I think it's the opposite. I think the larger a woman's breasts are, the less intelligent the men become.
                    —*Anita Wise*

SHY   PERKY

Breaking Up

If you love someone, set them free. If they come back, they're probably broke.

—*Rhonda Dicksion*

I broke up with my boyfriend because he wanted to get married. I didn't want him to.

—*Rita Rudner*

Q: What do you do when your boyfriend walks out?
A: Shut the door.

—*Angela Martin*

Cats

Cats think about three things:
food, sex and nothing.
                    —*Adair Lara*

A cat by any other name is still a
sneaky little furball who poops
behind the couch.
                    —*T-shirt slogan*

I wonder what goes through his
mind when he sees us peeing in
his water bowl.
                    —*Penny Ward Moser*

I found out why cats drink out of
the toilet. My mother told me it's
because it's cold in there. And I'm
like: 'How did my mother know
that?'
                    —*Wendy Liebman*

Whatever you're doing—it's not as
important as playing with the cat.
                    —*T-shirt slogan*

Dogs come when they're called;
cats take a message and get back
to you.
                    —*Mary Bly*

Cats are smarter than dogs. You
can't teach eight cats to pull a sled.
                    —*T-shirt slogan*

By and large, people who enjoy
teaching animals to roll over will
find themselves happier with a
dog.
                    —*Barbara Holland*

Your cat will never threaten your
popularity by barking at three
in the morning. He won't attack
the mailman or eat the drapes,
although he may climb the drapes
to see how the room looks from
the ceiling.
                    —*Helen Powers*

I'm used to dogs. When you leave
them in the morning, they stick
their nose in the door crack and
stand there like a portrait until
you turn the key eight hours later.
A cat would never put up with
that kind of rejection. When you
returned, she'd stalk you until you
dozed off and then suck the air
out of your body.
                    —*Erma Bombeck*

Q: What do macrobiotic cats eat?
A: Brown mice.

—*Anonymous*

Kittens have different nutritional needs than adult cats. Consult with your veterinarian and then, for the good of your relationship with your cat, forget everything she tells you.

—*Nicole Hollander*

I'm Catholic. My mother and I were unpacking and she found my diaphragm. I had to tell her it was a bathing cap for my cat.

—*Lizz Winstead*

Anything not nailed down is a cat toy.

—*T-shirt slogan*

Celibacy

No sex is better than bad sex.
—*Germaine Greer*

I've reached that point in life where you have to choose between happiness and getting laid. I'm happy.
—*Mary Frances Connelly*

It's been so long since I made love, I can't even remember who gets tied up.
—*Joan Rivers*

So many men and so many reasons not to sleep with any of them.
—*T-shirt slogan*

If they can put a man on the moon
why can't they put one in me?
—*Flash Rosenberg*

To me, the term "sexual freedom"
meant freedom from having to
have sex.
—*Lily Tomlin/Jane Wagner*

I SLEEP WITH MY TEDDY BEAR BECAUSE I KNOW WHERE HE'S BEEN.

Celebrities

Michael Jackson—he started life as a black man; now he's a white girl.
—*Mary Frances Connelly*

There's a broad with her future behind her.
—*Constance Bennett*
(about Marilyn Monroe)

Such an active lass. So outdoorsy. She loves nature in spite of what it did to her.
—*Bette Midler*
(about Princess Anne)

Sinead O'Connor: love child of John Cardinal O'Connor and Sandra Day O'Connor…
—*Kate Clinton*

Children

We are all God's children—by a previous marriage.

—*T-shirt slogan*

Never allow your child to call you by your first name. He hasn't known you long enough.

—*Fran Lebowitz*

Kids are like husbands—they're fine as long as they're someone else's.

—*Marsha Warfield*

Children ask better questions than adults. 'May I have a cookie?' 'Why is the sky blue?' and 'What does a cow say?' are far more likely to elicit a cheerful response than 'Where's your manuscript?' 'Why haven't you called?' and 'Who's your lawyer?'

—*Fran Lebowitz*

I met this guy who said he loved children, then I found out he was on parole for it.

Monica Piper

I want to have children while my parents are still young enough to take care of them.

—*Rita Rudner*

Ask your child what he wants for dinner only if he's buying.

—*Fran Lebowitz*

Notoriously insensitive to subtle shifts in mood, children will persist in discussing the color of a recently sighted cement mixer long after one's own interest in the topic has waned.

—*Fran Lebowitz*

Can you remember when you didn't want to sleep? Isn't it inconceivable? I guess the definition of adulthood is that you *want* to sleep.

—*Paula Poundstone*

Coffee

The only thing better than Great Sex…is Great Coffee!
—*Stephanie Piro*

Coffee is my only real friend.
—*Graffiti*

Never drink black coffee at lunch; it will keep you awake in the afternoon.
—*Jilly Cooper*

Behind every succcessful woman…is a substantial amount of coffee.
—*Stephanie Piro*

Complaints

I personally believe we developed
language because of our deep
inner need to complain.

—*Jane Wagner*

I have a *carpe diem* mug and,
truthfully, at six in the morning
the words do not make me want
to seize the day. They make me
want to slap a dead poet.

—*Joanne Sherman*

Communication

The only thing I ever said to my parents when I was a teenager was "Hang up, I got it!"

—*Carol Leifer*

Choose your words with taste. You may have to eat them.

—*Graffiti*

Ask me about my vow of silence.

—*T-shirt slogan*

Think 'Honk' if you're a telepath.

—*Bumpersticker*

Legislators do not merely mix metaphors: they are the Waring blenders of metaphors, the Cuisinarts of the field. By the time you let the head of the camel into the tent, opening a loophole big enough to drive a truck through, you may have thrown the baby out with the bathwater by putting a Band-Aid on an open wound, and then you have to turn over the first rock in order to find a sacred cow.

—*Molly Ivins*

My grandmother's 90. She's dating. He's 93. It's going great. They never argue. They can't hear each other.

—*Cathy Ladman*

A sentence is a fine thing to put a preposition at the end of.

—*T-shirt slogan*

Talk is cheap. Until you hire a lawyer.

—*Anonymous*

Anything you say will be distorted and remixed and used against you.

—*Anonymous*

Computers

Q: How can you tell when a dumb man's been using the wordprocessor?
A: There's whiteout on the screen.
　　　　—Girl Jock Magazine

Asking if computers can think is like asking if submarines can swim.
　　　　—T-shirt slogan

Abandon Hope, Ye Who Press Enter Here.
　　　　—Graffiti

Artificial Intelligence? I'll be impressed when they invent artificial cunning!
　　　　—T-shirt slogan

Cosmetic Surgery

A forty-five-year-old woman who
has had a face lift doesn't look
twenty-five. If it works, she looks
like a well-rested forty-three year
old woman. If it doesn't work, she
looks like a Halloween costume.
—*Fran Lebowitz*

FRIGE-O-SUCTION
The thought of surgery
to suck fat out of my body makes
    me feel sick.
I could never do it.
Instead of Liposuction,
why not go directly to the source?
I'd rather have FRIGE-O-SUCTION.
Please. Instead of needless surgery
just suck the food right out of my
    refrigerator
before it even lands on me.
—*Flash Rosenberg*

I don't plan to grow old gracefully.
I plan to have face-lifts till my ears
meet.

—*Rita Rudner*

If losing your head is a
be-heading, is liposuction a
be-hinding?

—*Flash Rosenberg*

SILICON VALLEY

Country & Western Music

I love the sound of Codependence
wafting over the prairie.

—*Carol Steinel*

Crime

I didn't steal this. It was
"differently acquired."
        —*Sara Cytron*

Cynicism

No matter how cynical you get, it's
impossible to keep up.
>—Lily Tomlin

Things are going to get a lot worse
before they get worse.
>—Lily Tomlin

Today is the first day of the wreck
of your life.
>—Becky Burke

The secret is to find out what
people really want and then call it
self-awareness.
>—T-shirt slogan

Two wrongs are only the beginning.
>—T-shirt slogan

Dating

Boys don't make passes at female
smart asses.

—*Letty Cottin Pogrebin*

I'd like to take you out—and leave
you there.

—*T shirt slogan*

How many of you ever started
dating someone because you were
too lazy to commit suicide?

—*Judy Tenuta*

MEN SELDOM
rub elbows
with girls
who wear
dildoes.

—*Chocolate Waters*

I've figured out why first dates
don't work any better than they
do. It's because they take place in
restaurants. Women are weird and
confused and unhappy about food,
and men are weird and confused
and unhappy about money, yet off
they go, the minute they meet, to
where you use money to buy food.

—*Adair Lara*

I'm not your type—I have a pulse.
> —*T-shirt slogan*

I'm dating the Pope. Actually I'm just using him to get to God.
> —*Judy Tenuta*

This guy says, "I'm perfect for you, 'cause I'm a cross between a macho and a sensitive man." I said, "Oh, a gay trucker?"
> —*Judy Tenuta*

Death

We're all cremated equal.

—*Jane Ace*

Support your local medical
examiner—die strangely.

—*T-shirt slogan*

They say you shouldn't say nothing
about the dead unless it's good.
He's dead. Good.

—*Moms Mabley*

Because I could not stop for death.
It kindly stopped for me—
Its subway rattle to my door
And I got on for free.

—*Lorraine Schein*

Definitions

Circular definition: see circular
definition.

> —*Anonymous*

Claustrophobia: fear of Santa
Claus.

> —*Anonymous*

Committee: a group that takes
minutes and wastes hours.

> —*Anonymous*

Hope is the feeling you have that
the feeling you have isn't
permanent.

> —*Jean Kerr*

London: a place you go to get bronchitis.
>—*Fran Lebowitz*

Purranoia: the fear that your cats are up to something.
>—*Anonymous*

Sleep is death without the responsibility.
>—*Fran Lebowitz*

—Diets & other Eating Disorders—

A waist is a terrible thing to mind.
> —*Jane Caminos*

I've decided that perhaps I'm bulimic and just keep forgetting to purge.
> —*Paula Poundstone*

Divorce

I never even believed in divorce
until after I got married.
                —*Diane Ford*

I still miss my ex-husband. (But
my aim is improving.)
                —*Anonymous*

The wages of sin is alimony.
                —*Carolyn Wells*

When I'm dating I look at a guy
and wonder, "Is this the man I
want my children to spend their
weekends with?"
                —*Rita Rudner*

Drugs

I said no to drugs but they didn't listen.

—*Graffiti*

A great many people in Los Angeles are on strict diets that restrict their intake of synthetic foods. The reason for this appears to be a widely-held belief that organically grown fruit and vegetables make the cocaine work faster.

—*Fran Lebowitz*

I'm not really happy—it's a chemical imbalance.

—*Anonymous*

No left turn unstoned.
—*Bumpersticker*

School-Free Drug Zone
—*Graffiti*

A drug is a substance that when injected into a lab rat produces a scientific paper.
—*Graffiti*

A friend of mine confused her valium with her birth control pills—she had 14 kids but she didn't give a shit.
—*Joan Rivers*

Dyslexia

Dyslexics of the world untie
> —*T-shirt slogan*

Dyslexics have more fnu.
> —*Graffiti*

Eccentrics

Ask me about my third
chromosome.
—*Bumpersticker*

He was the most self-involved guy
I ever met in my life. He had a
coffee mug on his table that said,
"I'm the greatest." He had a plaque
on the wall that said, "I'm number
one." And on his bedspread it
said, "The Best." In the middle of
making love he said, "Move
over—you're getting in my way."
—*Karen Haber*

I prefer to remain anomalous.
—*T-shirt slogan*

Ego

Listen, everyone is entitled to my opinion.

—*Madonna*

Question Authority. Ask me anything.

—*T-shirt slogan*

My superiority complex is bigger than your superiority complex.

—*T-shirt slogan*

Egotism—usually just a case of
mistaken nonentity.
—*Barbara Stanwyck*

I'm not shy. I'm studying my prey.
—*T-shirt slogan*

Success didn't spoil me; I've
always been insufferable.
—*Fran Lebowitz*

It takes a lot of time to be a
genius—you have to sit around
so much doing nothing, really
doing nothing.
—*Gertrude Stein*

Environment

The ozone layer or cheese in a
spray can? Don't make me choose!
   —*T-shirt slogan*

The other day I bought a wastebasket and carried it home in a paper
bag. And when I got home I put the
paper bag in the wastebasket.
   —*Lily Tomlin*

Experience

Keep a diary and one day it'll
keep you.

—*Mae West*

I'm the person your mother didn't
even dare mention.

—*T-shirt slogan*

A girl can wait for the right man to
come along but in the meantime
that still doesn't mean she can't
have a wonderful time with all the
wrong ones.

—*Cher*

I'm an experienced woman; I've
been around...Well, all right, I
might not've been around, but I've
been...nearby.

—*Mary Richards,*
"Mary Tyler Moore Show"

To err is human but it feels divine.

—*Mae West*

When women go wrong, men go right after them.

—*Mae West*

Girls who put out are tramps. Girls who don't are ladies. This is, however, a rather archaic usage of the word. Should one of you boys happen upon a girl who doesn't put out, do not jump to the conclusion that you have found a lady. What you have probably found is a lesbian.

—*Fran Lebowitz*

My heart is as pure as the driven slush.

—*Tallulah Bankhead*

Feminine Protection

Now they're advertising breathable
panty liners. You know some man
invented that product. No woman
would be inventing a panty liner
and putting little holes in there.
She'd put little tongues in there.
—*Diane Ford*

Fitness

My grandmother started walking
five miles a day when she was sixty.
She's ninety-three today and we
don't know where the hell she is.
—*Ellen Degeneres*

I don't think jogging is healthy,
especially morning jogging. If
morning joggers knew how
tempting they looked to morning
motorists, they would stay home
and do situps.
—*Rita Rudner*

They kept telling us we had to get
in touch with our bodies. Mine
isn't all that communicative but I
heard from it on Tuesday morning
when I genially proposed, "Body,
how'd you like to go to the nine
o'clock class in vigorous toning
with resistance?"

Clear as a bell my body
said, "Listen, bitch, do it and you
die."
—*Molly Ivins*

Outside every thin girl there's a fat man trying to get in.

—*Katherine Whitehorn*

There's a thin woman inside every fat woman. I ate mine.

—*Graffiti*

LOOK AT HAMSTERS —THEY EXERCISE ALL THE TIME — IS THAT HOW I WANT MY BODY?!

I've been doing leg lifts faithfully for about fifteen years, and the only thing that has gotten thinner is the carpet where I have been doing the leg lifts.

—*Rita Rudner*

Food

Food is an important part of a balanced diet.

—*Fran Lebowitz*

Breakfast cereals that come in the same colors as polyester leisure suits make oversleeping a virtue.

—*Fran Lebowitz*

I tried Flintstones vitamins. I didn't feel any better but I could stop the car with my feet.

—*Joan St. Onge*

I eat junk food to get it out of the house.

—*T-shirt slogan*

You've buttered your bread, now sleep in it.

—*Gracie Allen*

This recipe is certainly silly. It says to separate two eggs, but it doesn't say how far to separate them.

—*Gracie Allen*

It's so beautifully arranged on the plate—you know someone's fingers have been all over it.
        —*Julia Child*

When I buy cookies I just eat four and throw the rest away. But first I spray them with Raid so I won't dig them out of the garbage later. Be careful, though, because that Raid really doesn't taste that bad.
        —*Janette Barber*

Forget the withered rose
or faded vow from Mr. Right.
Love departs—but sauerkraut,
once savored, stays the night.
        —*Barbara J. Petoskey*

Skinny people piss me off. Especially when they say things like,'You know, sometimes I forget to eat.' Now I've forgotten my address, my mother's maiden name, my money, and my keys. But I've never forgotten to eat. You have to be a special kind of stupid to forget to eat. And fuck you! In that case, you don't *deserve* to eat.
        —*Marsha Warfield*

I was the toast of two continents:
Greenland and Australia.
—*Dorothy Parker*

Friendship

A friend is someone you don't have to talk to anymore once the food is on the table.

—*Sabrina Matthews*

Laugh and the world laughs with you. Cry and you cry with your girlfriends.

—*Laurie Kuslansky*

When I was a girl I only had two friends, and they were imaginary. And they would only play with each other.

—*Rita Rudner*

My true friends have always given me that supreme proof of devotion, a spontaneous aversion for the man I loved.

—*Colette*

Q: What can you give a friend who has everything?
A: Shelves.

—*Patty Marx*

Fun

Instant gratification takes too long.
—*Carrie Fisher*

If only we'd stop trying to be happy we could have a pretty good time.
—*Edith Wharton*

A desire to have all the fun is nine-tenths of the law of chivalry.
—*Dorothy Sayers*

When my cats aren't happy, I'm not happy. Not because I care about their mood but because I know they're just sitting there thinking up ways to get even.
—*Penny Ward Moser*

Too much of a good thing can be wonderful.
—*Mae West*

Games

Whenever you're holding all the
cards, why does everyone else turn
out to be playing chess?
—T-shirt slogan

It's not who wins or loses, it's who
keeps score.
—T-shirt slogan

It's not whether you win or lose—
it's how you lay the blame.
—Fran Lebowitz

The lottery—you have to play to
lose.
—T-shirt slogan

I figure you have the same chance
of winning the lottery whether
you play or not.
—Fran Lebowitz

Garb

I'll wear any color as long as its black.
> —*T-shirt slogan*

Never wear a hat that has more character than you do.
> —*T-shirt slogan*

If gentlemen prefer Hanes, why don't they wear them?
> —*Judith Sloan*

Style is contrast: firm, man-made breasts with a soft, cashmere cardigan.

—*Nora Dunn*

Q: Is lesbian dating an oxymoron?
A: No, but lesbian fashion is!

—*Lea Delaria*

I do not believe in God. I believe in cashmere.

—*Fran Lebowitz*

Excuse me while I change into something more formidable.

—*T-shirt slogan*

Fashion tells us that women's bodies are not supposed to be shaped like women's bodies, except during sex.

—*Julia Willis*

My sister has a social conscience now. She still wears her fur coat, but across the back she's embroidered a sampler that says "Rest in Peace."

—*Julia Willis*

If God had meant us to be
naked, we would have been born
that way.
> —*T-shirt slogan*

It costs a lot of money to look
this cheap.
> —*Dolly Parton*

It's not true I had nothing on. I
had the radio on.
> —*Marilyn Monroe*

A child develops individuality
long before he develops taste. I
have seen my kid straggle into the
kitchen in the morning with
outfits that need only one acces-
sory: an empty gin bottle.
> —*Erma Bombeck*

Eternal nothingness is okay if
you're dressed for it.
> —*T-shirt slogan*

Is it okay to hate men but dress just like them?

—*Karen Ripley*

Your right to wear a mint-green polyester leisure suit ends where it meets my eye.

—*Fran Lebowitz*

I miss the good old days when guys wore open shirts, gold chains and polyester suits. I met many men I was attracted to. Okay, so it *was* static cling...

—*Karen Silver*

If it were strictly up to me, I wouldn't get within a mile of a dress. My twin's the same way: Her husband had to *marry* her to get her to put on a dress, and it lasted 40 minutes—she brought jeans rolled up in her purse to the chapel.

—*Adair Lara*

This wedding dress cost almost $2,000. You're supposed to wear it once? Bullshit! I wear it to work, to the toilet...

—*Claudia Sherman*

Gender

The main difference between men and women is that men are lunatics and women are idiots.
—*Rebecca West*

As far as I'm concerned, being any gender is a drag.
—*Patti Smith*

If you want something said, ask a man. If you want something done, ask a woman.
—*Margaret Thatcher*

Scratch an actor—and you'll find an actress.
—*Dorothy Parker*

Gossip

If you can't say anything good about someone, sit right here by me.

—*Alice Roosevelt Longsworth*

I hate to spread rumors—but what else can one do with them?

—*Amanda Lear*

If it's any of your business, it isn't really gossip.

—*T-shirt slogan*

Grandmothers

My grandmother was a very tough
woman. She buried three husbands.
Two of them were just napping.
                —*Rita Rudner*

Gynecology

I got a postcard from my gynecologist. It said "Did you know it's
time for your annual check-up?"
No, but now my *mailman* does.
> —*Cathy Ladman*

The gynecologist says, "Relax,
relax, I can't get my hand out,
relax." I wonder why I'm not
relaxed. My feet are in the stir-
rups, my knees are in my face, and
the door is open facing me…And
my gynecologist does jokes! "Dr.
Schwartz at your cervix!" "I'm
dilated to meet you!" "Say ahhh."
"There's Jimmy Hoffa!" There's no
way you can get back at that son
of a bitch unless you learn to
throw your voice.
> —*Joan Rivers*

Gynecologist: Now I'm inserting
   the speculum…Isn't that a
   healthy pink cervix?…Would
   you like me to get a hand
   mirror so you can see it?
Patient: No! I don't even like to
   look at my *face* in the mirror.
> —*Lea Delaria*

Hair

I'm worried that my hair is going to get bigger than I am and take me places I don't want to go...

—*Jennifer Heath*

The heck with the natural look. After all, you can't take credit for what you're born with, only for what you do yourself. Where would Marilyn Monroe be if she'd clung to the hair color God gave her? We'd have a movie called "Gentlemen Prefer Mousy Brown Hair."

—*Adair Lara*

Q: What request are you unlikely to make to your hairdresser in this lifetime?
A: Do my hair like Marilyn Quayle's.

—*Nicole Hollander*

I happen to have weird hair which is why I don't dress up fancy. If I dress up, people just look at me and go, 'Oooh, look at her head.' This way here, it's more of a total look and nobody can put their finger on quite what they think is wrong.

—*Paula Poundstone*

HAIR OBEDIENCE SCHOOL

THESE ARE ONLY A SAMPLE OF COMMANDS YOU'LL LEARN.

STAY!   ROLL OVER!   DOWN!   FETCH!

TRAIN YOUR HAIR FAST! TRAIN WIGS, TOUPÉES, NOSE HAIR, EAR HAIR, HAIR BALLS.

Halloween

A fine American tradition of
teaching our children to beg door-
to-door dressed as mass murderers
and co-dependent women. The
planning takes weeks, but it's
worth it just to see how lively a
four-year-old can get after
mainstreaming Milk Duds for
three hours.

—*Cathy Crimmins*

Health

Health—what my friends are always drinking to before they fall down.

    —Phyllis Diller

Doctor: Did your parents enjoy good health?
Gracie Allen: Oh yes, they loved it.

Never go to a doctor whose office plants have died.

    —Erma Bombeck

Happiness is good health and a bad memory.

    —Ingrid Bergman

Hell

My idea of hell is to be stranded
on a desert island with nothing to
read but Anais Nin's diaries.
> —*Katha Pollitt*

There is no heaven or hell—only
smoking or non-smoking.
> —*Anonymous*

In hell all the messages you ever
left on answering machines will be
played back to you.
> —*Judy Horacek*

History

History repeats itself, but each
time the price goes up.

—*Graffiti*

Home

Home is a great place—after all
the other places have closed.
                    —*Texas Guinan*

Housekeeping

I'm a wonderful housekeeper.
Every time I get divorced, I keep
the house.

—*Zsa Zsa Gabor*

Don't cook. Don't clean. No man
will ever make love to a woman
because she waxed the linoleum—
"My God, the floor's immaculate.
Lie down, you hot bitch."

—*Joan Rivers*

A dish that don't survive the
dishwasher don't deserve to live.

—*Liz Scott*

I prefer the word homemaker,
because housewife always implies
that there may be a wife some-
place else.

—*Bella Abzug*

I don't buy temporary insanity as a
murder defense. Breaking into
someone's home and ironing all
their clothes is temporary insanity.

—*Sue Kolinsky*

I would rather lie on a sofa than sweep beneath it.

—*Shirley Conran*

Give me levity or give me death.

—*Graffiti*

Nature abhors a vacuum. And so do I.

—*Anne Gibbons*

Cleaning your home while your kids are still growing is like shoveling the walk before it stops snowing.

—*Phyllis Diller*

If you want to get rid of stinking odors in the kitchen, stop cooking.

—*Erma Bombeck*

Humor

If evolution was worth its salt, by now it should've evolved something better than survival of the fittest...I think a better idea would be survival of the wittiest.

—*Jane Wagner*

She who laughs, lasts.

—*Graffiti*

Humor is emotional chaos recalled in tranquility.

—*T-shirt slogan*

The women-and-wit conundrum came to a head in a 1976 book called *The Curse: A Cultural History of Menstruation* by Janice Delaney, Mary Jane Lupton and Emily Troth. In a chapter on menstruation jokes, this earnest trio came up with one of the finest oxymorons of all time: 'We would like to think that feminism will help women develop a different sense of humor, one that is warm, loving, egalitarian, compassionate.' That's like telling people to have calm orgasms.

—*Florence King*

Insults

You remind me of my brother Bosco—only he had a human head.

—*Judy Tenuta*

We all have to go sometime—why don't you go now?

—*Anonymous*

She's the original good time that was had by all.

—*Betty Davis*
(about another actress)

Don't let your mind wander. It's too little to be let out alone.

—*T-shirt slogan*

Were you standing at the shallow end of the gene pool?

—*T-shirt slogan*

Journalism

Journalism is the ability to meet
the challenge of filling space.
    —*Rebecca West*

You should always believe all you
read in the newspapers, as this
makes them more interesting.
    —*Rose Macaulay*

Justice

No good deed goes unpunished.
> —*Clare Boothe Luce*

Juries scare me. I don't want to put my fate in the hands of twelve people who weren't even smart enough to get out of jury duty.
> —*Monica Piper*

MIKE TYSON
Why was he sent to jail? A last resort.
No place was open on the Supreme Court.
> —*Katherine McAlpine*

George Bush and Ronald Reagan have insured their place in history through the legacy they have created in the Supreme Court. They have managed to appoint a misogynistic woman and an anti-civil rights African-American to the Court. They have, however, also contributed a new oxymoron to the English language: Supreme Court Justice.
> —*Jana Rivington*

In this world it rains on the Just and the Unjust, but the Unjust have the Just's Umbrella.
> —*T-shirt slogan*

Lawyers

I don't believe man is woman's
natural enemy. Perhaps his lawyer is.
—*Shana Alexander*

Laziness

I'm not slow—you're impatient.
> —*T-shirt slogan*

My mother told me, 'Judy, you'll never amount to anything because you always procrastinate.' I said, 'Oh yeah? Just wait!'
> —*Judy Tenuta*

I'm killing time, wasting space and going through a phase.
> —*T-shirt slogan*

I'm taking the scenic route through life.
> —*T-shirt slogan*

If only you could get that wonderful feeling of accomplishment without having to do anything.
> —*T-shirt slogan*

Don't hate yourself in the morning—
sleep till noon.
>
> —*T-shirt slogan*

I'm so laid back I fell off.
>
> —*T-shirt slogan*

Anything worth not doing is
worth not doing well.
>
> —*T-shirt slogan*

READING IN BED IS <u>NOT</u> ONE OF THE
SEVEN DEADLY SINS!

Lesbians & Gays

If space and time are curved, then where do all the straight people come from?

—*Anonymous*

Q: How do people get to be homosexual?

A: Homosexuals are chosen first on talent, then interview, and then the swimsuit and evening gown competitions...

—*Suzanne Westenhoefer*

My lesbianism is an act of Christian charity. All those women out there are praying for a man, and I'm giving them my share.

—*Rita Mae Brown*

I wear a T-shirt that says "The Family tree stops here."

—*Suzanne Westenhoefer*

I went out with a Chinese gentleman. He turned out to be gay. He took me to a Chinese restaurant called Sum Yung Guy.

—*Ellen Orchid*

I'm out, therefore I am.

—*Ursula Roma*

What I Love About Lesbian Politics
Is Arguing With People I Agree With
(book title)
          —*Kris Kovick*

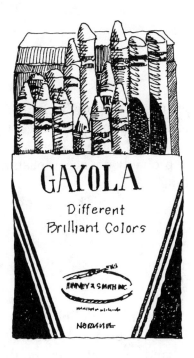

"I'll be a Homo For Christmas"—
(song title)
         —*Lisa Koch,* Venus Envy

GAYOLA

Different
Brilliant Colors

Q: What do lesbians do in bed?
A: It's a lot like heterosexual sex,
only one of us doesn't have to fake
orgasm.
        —*Suzanne Westenhoefer*

I'd rather have a bigot think I'm a
lesbian than a lesbian think I'm a
bigot.
        —*T-shirt slogan*

Q; What do you call a lesbian who dates men?
A: I call her Holly Near.
—*Lea Delaria*

All women are lesbians, except those who don't know it yet.
—*Jill Johnston*

A lesbian is any uppity woman, regardless of sexual preference. If they don't call you a lesbian, you're probably not accomplishing anything.
—*Cheris Kramarae & Paula Treichler*

I was so excited to be able to say that I was a lesbian that I would shake hands with strangers on the street and say, 'Hi! I'm Sally Gearhart and I'm a lesbian.' Once, appearing on a panel program, I began, 'I'm Sally Lesbian and I'm a Gearhart!' I realized then that I had put too much of my identity into being a lesbian.
—*Sally Gearhart*

BREAST SELF-EXAMS MADE ME GAY!

* FINALLY I REALIZED EVERYTIME I MASTURBATED: HEY! I'm MAKING LOVE TO A WOMAN!"

Life

Life is something to do when you can't get to sleep.
> —*Fran Lebowitz*

If I had to live my life again, I'd make all the same mistakes—only sooner.
> —*Tallulah Bankhead*

The average, well-adjusted adult gets up at 7:30 in the morning feeling just terrible.
> —*Jean Kerr*

Don't take life seriously—it isn't permanent.
> —*T-shirt slogan*

I used to get high on life but I've built up a tolerance.
> —*T-shirt slogan*

They say the movies should be
more like life. I think life should
be more like the movies.
>—*Myrna Loy*

My life is based on a true story.
>—*T-shirt slogan*

It is not true that life is one damn
thing after another—it's one damn
thing over and over.
>—*Edna St. Vincent Millay*

Life is a glorious cycle of song,
A medley of extemporania;
And love is a thing that can never
go wrong,
And I am Marie of Rumania.
>—*Dorothy Parker*

Life's a beach and then you dry.
>—*Graffiti*

Literature

You can't judge a book by its movie.

> —*T-shirt slogan*

The difference between owning a book and borrowing a book is that when you own it you can get food on it.

> —*Susan Catherine*

Outside of a dog, a book is your
best friend, and inside of a dog, it's
too dark to read.
> —*T-shirt slogan*

I have only read one book in my
life, and that is *White Fang*. It's so
frightfully good I've never both-
ered to read another.
> —*Nancy Mitford*

This is not a novel to be tossed
lightly aside. It should be thrown
with great force.
> —*Dorothy Parker*

Love

One of the surest signs that a
woman is in love is when she
divorces her husband.
>—*Anonymous*

Love conquers all things except
poverty and a toothache.
>—*Mae West*

If love is the answer could you
please rephrase the question?
>—*Lily Tomlin*

Make-up

Make-up is such a weird concept, but I buy into it like every woman I know. I'll wake up in the morning and look in the mirror: "Gee, I really don't look so good. Maybe if my eyelids were blue, I'd be more attractive…"

—*Cathy Ladman*

Marriage

The trouble with some women is that they get all excited about nothing—and then marry him.

—*Cher*

The only thing that keeps me from being happily married…is my husband.

—*Andra Douglas*

Bigamy is having one husband too many. Monogamy is the same.

—*Erica Jong*

The surest way to be alone is to get married.

—*Gloria Steinem*

I TRIED TO DROWN MY THOUGHTS
BUT THEY LEARNED HOW TO SWIM.

Getting married is a lot like getting into a tub of hot water. After you get used to it, it ain't so hot.

—*Minnie Pearl*

I married the first man I ever kissed. When I tell my children that, they just about throw up.

—*Barbara Bush*

Marrying a man is like buying something you've been admiring for a long time in a shop window. You may love it when you get it home, but it doesn't always go with everything else.

—*Jean Kerr*

My parents want me to get married. They don't care who anymore as long as he doesn't have a pierced ear, that's all they care about. I think men who have a pierced ear are better prepared for marriage. They've experienced pain and bought jewelry.

—*Rita Rudner*

Any woman who still thinks marriage is a fifty-fifty proposition is only proving that she doesn't understand either men or percentages.

—*Flo Kennedy*

Marriage is a great institution, but
I'm not ready for an institution yet.
                    —*Mae West*

Some of us are becoming the men
we wanted to marry.
                    —*Gloria Steinem*

I married beneath me—all
women do.
                    —*Nancy Astor*

A man in love is incomplete until
he's married—then he's finished.
                    —*Zsa Zsa Gabor*

The old theory was "Marry an
older man, because they're more
mature." But the new theory is:
"Men don't mature. Marry a
younger one."
                    —*Rita Rudner*

I'm 33, single... Don't you think
it's a generalization you should be
married at 33? That's like looking
at somebody who's 70 and saying
'Hey, when are you gonna break
your hip? All your friends are
breaking their hips—what are you
waiting for?
                    —*Sue Kolinsky*

I haven't known any open
marriages, though quite a few
have been ajar.
                —Zsa Zsa Gabor

George, you're too old to get
married again. Not only can't you
cut the mustard, honey, you're too
old to open the jar.
                —La Wanda Page,
                    to George Burns

Trust your husband, adore your
husband, and get as much as you
can in your own name.
                —Joan Rivers

When marriage is outlawed, only
outlaws will have in-laws.
                —T-shirt slogan

I can't mate in captivity.
        —Gloria Steinem, when asked
            why she had never married

Men

Personally, I think if a woman hasn't met the right man by the time she's 24, she may be lucky.
—*Deborah Kerr*

Ninety-nine percent of men give the other one percent a bad name.
—*Anonymous*

You know, all that stuff I call men—'hot slabs of meat,' 'love slaves,' 'pigs'—that's all affectionate.
—*Judy Tenuta*

A good man doesn't just happen. They have to be created by us women. A guy is a lump like a doughnut. So, first you gotta get rid of all the stuff his mom did to him, and then you gotta get rid of all that macho crap that they pick up from the beer commercials. And then there's my personal favorite, the male ego.
—*Roseanne Arnold*

Women want mediocre men, and men are working hard to be as mediocre as possible.
—*Margaret Mead*

Macho does not prove mucho.
—*Zsa Zsa Gabor*

It is possible that blondes also prefer gentlemen.
—*Mamie Van Doren*

Q: When did God create men?
A: When she realized that vibrators couldn't dance or buy drinks.
—*Anonymous*

A woman is a woman until the day she dies, but a man's a man only as long as he can.
—*Moms Mabley*

Gay, straight...they all want blow jobs.
—*Graffiti*

If they can put one man on the moon why can't they put them all there?
—*Chocolate Waters*

Q: Can you imagine a world without men?
A: No crime, and lots of happy fat women.
—*Nicole Hollander*

Men Drivers

Q: Why is the track at the INDY
   500 an oval?
A: So men won't have to stop and
   ask for directions.

—*Anonymous*

Basically, my husband has two
beliefs in life. He believes in God,
and he believes that when the gas
gauge is on empty, he still has a
quarter of a tank. He thinks the
"E" stands for "Eeeggghh, there's
still some left."

—*Rita Rudner*

How many roads must a man
travel down before he admits he
is lost?

—*T-shirt slogan*

Men can read maps better than women. 'Cause only the male mind could conceive of one inch equaling a hundred miles.
—*Roseanne Arnold*

Don't accept rides from strange men—and remember that all men are strange as hell.
—*Robin Morgan*

Menopause

They're not hot flashes—they're power surges!

—*T-shirt slogan*

Why do they call it menopause and not menostop? And what do men have to do with it anyway?

—*Karen Ripley*

SUPER MA'AM

Menstruation

A period is just the beginning of a lifelong sentence.

> —*Cathy Crimmins*

Every month he asks me if I've got 'the curse'…So, finally I told him, 'I must, I'm living with you, aren't I…?'

> —*Stephanie Piro*

I would like it if men had to partake in the same hormonal cycles to which we're subjected monthly. Maybe that's why men declare war—because they have a need to bleed on a regular basis.

> —*Brett Butler*

I've been sort of crabby lately. It's that time of month again—the rent's due.

> —*Margaret Smith*

Q: What's the difference between worry and panic?
A: About twenty-eight days.

> —*Anonymous*

Mid-life Crisis

The cup isn't half empty—it's evaporating!

—*Alice Kahn*

The mid-life crisis usually begins with a checkup at the doctor's. You feel you are in perfect health. And you are. It's just that you suddenly realize the doctor is some punk kid. You can no longer call him Dr. Silverstein. Instead, you say, "Do you know a damn thing about systemic yeast, Sean?"

—*Alice Kahn*

Mood

I'm apathetic and I don't care.
>   —*Graffiti*

>   I'm marching to a different kettle
>   of fish.
>   —*Graffiti*

Money

I do want to get rich but I never want to do what there is to do to get rich.

—*Gertrude Stein*

I don't want to make money. I just want to be wonderful.

—*Marilyn Monroe*

Money is how people with no talent keep score.

—*Anonymous*

If this man had not twelve thousand a year, he would be a very stupid fellow.

—*Jane Austen*

The most beautiful words in the English language are "check enclosed."
—*Dorothy Parker*

I don't buy all this news of a rebounding economy. Just the other day my best friend had a nose job—and 12 people applied.
—*Mary Jo Crowley*

Money is always there, but the pockets change.
—*Gertrude Stein*

I believe we should all pay our tax bill with a smile. I tried—but they wanted cash.
—*Graffiti*

Motherhood

The way I look at it, if the kids are still alive when my husband comes home from work, then I've done my job.

—*Roseanne Arnold*

Never lend your car to anyone to whom you have given birth.

—*Erma Bombeck*

A woman came to ask the doctor if a woman should have children after 35. I said 35 children is enough for any woman!

—*Gracie Allen*

I was on a corner the other day when a wild-looking sort of gypsy-looking lady with a dark veil over her face grabbed me right on Ventura Boulevard and said, "Karen Haber! You're never going to find happiness, and no one is ever going to marry you." I said, "Mom, leave me alone."

—*Karen Haber*

It's not easy being a mother. If it
were easy, fathers would do it.
  —Dorothy, "The Golden Girls"

Children use up the same part of
my head as poetry does.
  —Libby Houston

My mother says she just wants me
to be happy—doing what she
wants me to do.
                    —*Julia Willis*

Mothers always tell you that
honesty is the best policy, and
money isn't everything. They're
wrong about other things, too.
                    —*Graffiti*

I don't have any kids. Well…at
least none that I know about.
                    —*Carol Leifer*

The phrase 'working mother' is
redundant.
                    —*Jane Sellman*

Never have more children than
you have car windows.
                    —*Erma Bombeck*

Mother's Day

What do you get on Mother's Day
if you have kids? You know what.
A card with flowers that are made
out of pink toilet paper—a lot of
pink toilet paper. You get breakfast in bed. Then you get up and
fix everybody else their breakfast.
And then you go to the bathroom,
and you are out of toilet paper.

—*Liz Scott*

New Age

Q: What do you get when you play
   New Age Music backwards?
A: New Age Music.
> —*Anonymous*

The New Age is just like the old
age—only newer.
> —*T-shirt slogan*

The New Age is getting older but
shows no signs of wising up.
> —*Alice Kahn*

Out of Body. Back in 5 Minutes.
> —*T-shirt slogan*

It's ll o'clock—do you know where
your chakras are?
> —*Julia Willis*

Visualize World Wrestling.
> —*T-shirt slogan*

Penises

If brevity is the soul of wit, your penis must be a riot.
> —*Donna Gephart*

When I was in third grade, there was a kid running for office. His slogan was: 'Vote for me and I'll show you my wee-wee.' He won by a landslide.
> —*Dorothy, "The Golden Girls"*

Okay the joke is over—show me your real penis!
> —*T-shirt slogan*

Q: What do you get when you cross a penis with a potato?
A: A dictator.
> —*Girl Jock Magazine*

I don't sleep with men who've named their dicks.
> —*T-shirt slogan*

I don't know, darling—he never sucked *my* cock.
— *Tallulah Bankhead, asked if an acquaintance was gay*

Freud and Jung broke up over the concept of penis envy. Freud thought that every woman wanted a penis. Jung thought that every woman wanted *his* penis.
—*Ellen Orchid*

Let's forget about the six feet and talk about the seven inches.
—*Mae West, on being told that a new male acquaintance was 6' 7".*

On the Phil Donahue Show I saw that many men were impotent. How many men *here* are impotent?…Oh, you can't get your hands up either?
—*Roseanne Arnold*

Philosophy

There's not much good in the worst of us, and so many of the worst of us get the best of us, that the rest of us aren't even worth talking about.

—*Gracie Allen*

Sometimes I worry about being a success in a mediocre world.

—*Lily Tomlin*

Ignorance is no excuse—it's the real thing.

—*Irene Peter*

I do whatever my Rice Krispies tell me to do.

—*T-shirt slogan*

If you're going to walk on thin ice, you might as well dance.

—*T-shirt slogan*

EXISTENTIALISM I
I wanted to write this poem
eons ago,
but forgot what it was about.
Now that I remember,
here it is.

—*Nicole S. Urdang*

Complex problems have simple, easy to understand, wrong answers.
>
> —*T-shirt slogan*

It is better to trip and end up on the floor, than to not trip and end up on the floor for no particular reason.
>
> —*T-shirt slogan*

My Karma Ran Over My Dogma
>
> —*T-shirt slogan*

I had never been as resigned to ready-made ideas as I was to ready-made clothes, perhaps because although I couldn't sew, I could think.
>
> —*Jane Rule*

Ignorance is bliss but it'll never replace sex.
>
> —*T-shirt slogan*

If you can keep your head while all about you are losing theirs, it's just possible you haven't grasped the situation.
>
> —*Jean Kerr*

— Phones & Answering Machines —

We don't care. We don't have to.
We're the phone company.
   —Lily Tomlin, as Ernestine

Hi, This is Sylvia. I can't come to the
phone right now, so when you hear
the beep, please hang up (book title)
   —Nicole Hollander

PHONE ECONOMICS
Even though I don't have any
 money, I NEVER worry
about how much it costs to talk
 on the phone
because I go by The Theory of
 Flash Phone Economics:
As far as I'm concerned it's ALL
 FREE
…except for one day.
One really BAD day
…when I have to pay the bill.
   —Flash Rosenberg

PMS

My doctor said 'I've got good news
and I got bad news. The good
news is you don't have Premen-
strual Syndrome. The bad news
is—you're a bitch!'
　　　　　　—*Rhonda Bates*

THE PMS PRAYER
God grant me the serenity
to change the things about me
　　and others
I cannot stand
And to stand the things about me
　　and others
I cannot change
And the insight to know the
　　difference
Between a PMS day and a
　　normal day
So no one gets hurt.
　　　　　　—*Susan Hankla*

My license plate says PMS.
Nobody cuts me off.
　　　　　　—*Wendy Liebman*

Poetry

Poets should be paid for their work, just like politicians and sports announcers and other people who produce verbiage that nobody wants to hear. They should get a pension from the state so that they can produce poetry without starving. In fact, no one should be eligible for welfare without being able to prove that he or she is writing poetry.

—*Gail White*

IF EQUAL AFFECTION CANNOT BE...

☐ LET THE MORE LOVING ONE BE ME.
☐ LET THE MORE LOVING ONE BE YOU.
☐ LET THE MORE CO-DEPENDENT ONE BE ME.
☐ LET THE MORE SADISTIC ONE BE ME.

Politics

All politicians are alligators; they are *all* alligators.

—*Billie Carr*

This country is run by men. Need I say more?

—*T-shirt slogan*

A fool and his money are soon elected.

—*Anonymous*

The great quadrennial national circus is upon us: three rings, cast of thousands, red, white, and blue balloons by the ton, red, white, and blue bullshit by the hour, confusion, exhaustion, alcohol, and the fate of the nation.

—*Molly Ivins*

If God had wanted us to vote, she would have given us candidates.

—*graffiti*

As far as the men who are running for president are concerned, they aren't even people I would date.
—*Nora Ephron*

Calling George Bush shallow is like calling a dwarf short.
—*Molly Ivins*

A politician is a fellow who will lay down your life for his country.
—*Texas Guinan*

The press went tearing off down a very dangerous and stupid path in '88 when they wrote about Hart's affairs. After twenty-five years of watching politics I have never been able to cite any correlation whatever between who these guys screw and how they perform in public office. The question is who they screw in their public capacity.
—*Molly Ivins*

Ninety-eight percent of the adults in this country are decent, hard-working, honest Americans. It's the other lousy two percent that get all the publicity. But then we elected them.
—*Lily Tomlin*

Bureaucrats cut red tape—
lengthwise.
>—*T-shirt slogan*

Part of Bush's problem is that he is
not a well-educated man. He just
went to good schools.
>—*Molly Ivins*

No matter who you vote for, the
government gets elected.
>—*T-shirt slogan*

A woman's place is in the house,
the senate, and the oval office.
>—*Anonymous*

I am working for the time when
unqualified blacks, browns and
women join the unqualified men
in running our government.
>—*Cissy Farenthold*

Real Texans do not use the word
"summer" as a verb. Real Texans
do not wear blue slacks with little
green whales all over them. And
real Texans never refer to trouble
as 'deep doo-doo.'
>—*Molly Ivins*

A female president—maybe they'd
start calling it the 'Ova Office.'
 —*Brett Butler*

If you want help from the United
States government—move to
another country!
 —*Anonymous*

Foreign aid is the transfer of
money from poor people in rich
countries to rich people in poor
countries.
 —*T-shirt slogan*

Politically correct is a contradiction
in terms.
 —*Anonymous*

There's one sure way of telling
when politicans are telling the
truth—their lips move.
 —*Felicity Kendal*

Porn

My reaction to porno films is as follows: After the first ten minutes, I want to go home and screw. After the first twenty minutes, I never want to screw again as long as I live.

—*Erica Jong*

Men love looking at pictures of two naked women together in their *Penthouses*—but only if they're pretty. You get ol' Marge and Madge stepping out of a big rig after a long day in the seat, and guys are like, "Hey! That ain't natural."

—*Brett Butler*

Pregnancy & Childbirth

If pregnancy were a book, they would cut the last two chapters.
—*Nora Ephron*

"Feel the baby kicking, feel the baby kicking," says my friend who is six minutes pregnant and deliriously happy about it. To me, life is tough enough without having someone kick you from the inside.
—*Rita Rudner*

"You're Having My Baby—What a Lovely Way To Say That You Are Stupid." (song title)
—*Judy Tenuta*

He tricked me into marrying him. He told me I was pregnant.
—*Carol Leifer*

When I had my baby, I screamed and screamed. And that was just during conception.
—*Joan Rivers*

I told my mother I was going to have natural childbirth. She said to me, 'Linda, you've been taking drugs all your life. Why stop now?'
—*Linda Maldonado*

When I was born, I was so surprised
I couldn't talk for a year and a half.
—*Gracie Allen*

One of my friends told me she was
in labor for thirty-six hours. I
don't even want to do anything
that feels *good* for thirty-six hours.
—*Rita Rudner*

One book recommends choosing a
Birth Mantra to chant over and
over again. I didn't realize until I
went into labor that I had subcon-
sciously chosen my mantra: "Get
This Baby Out Of Me."
—*Cathy Crimmins*

Pregnancy is much like adolescence, except it's more tiring and you don't get to leave home when it's over.
—*Cathy Crimmins*

When I was in labor the nurses would look at me and say, "Do you still think blondes have more fun?'"
—*Joan Rivers*

When a friend gave birth to a child, Dorothy Parker sent her a congratulatory telegram: "We All Knew You Had It In You!"
—*Anonymous*

When I was five years old my mother told me that when you fell in love and decided to have a baby, that's when you asked God and God sent you a baby—which is essentially how lesbians have their babies, if you think of God as a sperm bank.
—*Julia Willis, Who Wears TheTux?*

Race & Ethnicity

Men look at me and think I'm going to walk on their backs or something. I tell them the only time I'll walk on your back is if there's something on the other side of you that I want.
—*Margaret Cho*

I think we can agree racial prejudice is stupid. Because if you spend time with someone from another race and really get to know them, you can find other reasons to hate them.
—*Bernadette Luckett*

I travel a lot, and every day I'm in a different hotel. For some reason people mistake me for the maid. The other day this guy says, 'You can come into my room and do your job now!' So I went in there and told him some jokes.
—*Dr. Bertice Berry,*
stand-up comic

There is an incredible amount of magic and feistiness in black men that nobody has been able to wipe out. But everybody has tried.
—*Toni Morrison*

I don't look like Whoopi Goldberg. People confuse us because we're both Black and have dreadlocks. The other day a lady on the bus said to me, 'You look just like Whoopi Goldberg.' I told her, 'You're fat and White, but you don't look like Mama Cass!'"
—*Dr. Bertice Berry*

My mother's Puerto Rican and my father's Russian-Jewish so we consider ourselves to be Jewricans or Puertojews. I think Puertojew sounds like a kosher bathroom, so I prefer Jewrican.
—*Rachel Ticotin*

I grew up in Concord, Massachu-setts, and we were the only black family there. So, you know when a subject comes up that may include you, people tend to stare at you? Well, whenever they'd talk about Africa when I was in school, every-one would turn around and stare at me like I suddenly got a spear in my hand.
—*Angela Scott*

Rage

Never go to bed mad. Stay up and fight.

—*Phyllis Diller*

I read one psychologist's theory that said, 'Never strike a child in anger.' When could I strike him? When he's kissing me on my birthday? When he is recuperating from measles? Do I slap the Bible out of his hand on a Sunday?

—*Erma Bombeck*

God grant me the serenity to accept things I cannot change, the courage to change the things I can and the weaponry to make the difference.

—*Anonymous*

Reality

I made some studies, and reality is
the leading cause of stress
amongst those in touch with it.
—*Jane Wagner*

I live in another dimension but I
have a summer home in reality.
—*Anonymous*

My reality check just bounced.
—*Anonymous*

In city rooms and in the bars
where newspeople drink, you can
find out what's going on. You can't
find it in the papers.
—*Molly Ivins*

Religion

I recently became a Christian Scientist. It was the only health plan I could afford.

—*Betsy Salkind*

Jesus is coming—look busy!

—*T-shirt slogan*

God is love, but get it in writing.

—*Gypsy Rose Lee*

I happen to be a devout atheist. I don't believe in God. I still go to church—I'm not a heathen. I go to an atheist church. We have crippled guys who stand up and testify that they were crippled, and they still are.

—*Paula Poundstone*

Militant Agnostic—I don't know and you don't know either!

—*T-shirt slogan*

I found Jesus. He said "Tag—
you're it!"

—*Graffiti*

Jeez if you love Honkus.

—*Bumpersticker*

All religions are the same. Religion
is basically guilt, with different
holidays.

—*Cathy Ladman*

I went to a convent in New York
and was fired finally for my
insistence that the Immaculate
Conception was spontaneous
combustion.

—*Dorothy Parker*

Q: How do you explain human
suffering if there is a God?
A: Shouldn't God be the one
explaining?

—*Patricia Marx*

You'll go to Heck if you don't
believe in Gosh.

—*T-shirt slogan*

When we talk to God, we're
praying. When God talks to us,
we're schizophrenic.

—*Jane Wagner*

Frisbeetarianism —the belief that
when you die, your soul goes up
on the roof and gets stuck.

—*T-shirt slogan*

Anita Bryant is to Christianity
what paint-by-numbers is to Art.

—*Robin Tyler*

Romance

If you can't live without me, why aren't you dead yet? (book title)
—*Cynthia Heimel*

Cinderella lied to us. There should be a Betty Ford Center where they deprogram you by putting you in an electric chair, play "Some Day My Prince Will Come" and hit you and go "Nobody's coming... Nobody's coming...Nobody's coming..."

—*Judy Carter*

Treat romance like a cane toad. Study it furtively—then squash it!
—*Kaz Cooke*

Rules

If you obey all the rules you miss all the fun.

—*Katharine Hepburn*

If you don't make the rules you don't have to keep them. If you do make the rules, you won't anyway.

—*T-shirt slogan*

The trouble with unwritten laws is that they're so difficult to erase.

—*T-shirt slogan*

Freedom is just chaos with better lighting.

—*T-shirt slogan*

School

I majored in nursing but I had to drop it because I ran out of milk.
—*Judy Tenuta*

Stand firm in your refusal to remain conscious during algebra. In real life, I assure you, there is no such thing as algebra.
—*Fran Lebowitz*

Science

New clinical studies show there are no answers.
—*T-shirt slogan*

The latest scientific studies show that *all* mice and rats have cancer.
—*Julia Willis*

The rings of Saturn are actually composed of lost airline luggage.
—*T-shirt slogan*

Gravity isn't my fault—I voted for velcro.
—*Graffiti*

The formula for water is H_2O. Is the formula for an ice cube H_2O squared?
—*Lily Tomlin*

I ♥ SCIENCE

Sex

A hard man is good to find.
—*Mae West*

A healthy sex life. Best thing in the world for a woman's voice.
—*Leontyne Price*

A little coitus wouldn't hoitus.
—*Graffiti*

Women complain about sex more often than men. Their gripes fall into two major categories: l) Not enough. 2) Too much.
—*Ann Landers*

I understand there's a new edition of Playboy Magazine designed for married men. Every month the centerfold is the same picture.
—*Mary Jo Crowley*

The important thing in acting is to be able to laugh and cry. If I have to cry, I think of my sex life. If I have to laugh, I think of my sex life.
—*Glenda Jackson*

Sex when you're married is like going to a 7-ll. There's not much variety but at three in the morning, it's always there.

—*Carol Leifer*

Q: Just how responsible am I for
   my partner's orgasm?
A: Well, I guess that depends on
   whether or not you're there.

—*Lea Delaria*

Nothing was happening in our marriage. I nicknamed our waterbed Lake Placid.

—*Phyllis Diller*

If men really knew how to do it,
they wouldn't have to pay for it.
—*Roseanne Arnold*

Dr. Ruth says we women should
tell our lovers how to make love to
us. My boyfriend goes nuts if I tell
him how to *drive*!
—*Pam Stone*

The male attitude toward sex is
like squirting jam into a doughnut.
—*Germaine Greer*

There are three kinds of sex in a
marriage: exciting sex, necessary
sex and hallway sex. Exciting sex is
when you're first married and you
can't wait to get at each other.
Necessary sex is after you've been
married for seven or eight years
and it's more of a chore than
anything else. Hallway sex is after
you've been married for thirty or
forty years and you pass each other
in the hallway and say *Fuck You*!
—*Susan Savannah*

There's a sucker born every minute. Swallowers are tougher to find.

—*T-shirt slogan*

He just kept rushing through the lovemaking. Which is the part I like, the beginning part. Most women are like that. We need time to warm up. Why is this hard for you guys to understand? You're the first people to tell *us* not to gun a cold engine. You want us to go from zero to sixty in a minute. We're not built like that. We stall.

—*Anita Wise*

Q: What do men really like in bed?
A: Breakfast.

—*Nicole Hollander*

You know why God is a man?
Because if God was a woman she
would have made sperm taste like
chocolate.

—*Carrie Snow*

Dating is hard on guys. Guys just
got really good lying about how
many women they have had and
now they have to lie about how
many women they haven't had.

—*Diane Ford*

I love the lines men use to get
us into bed. "Please, I'll only put
it in for a minute." What am I, a
microwave?

—*Beverly Mickins*

I feel like a million tonight—but
one at a time.

—*Mae West*

Sexual Harassment

Q: What's the difference between
    men and pigs?
A: Pigs don't get drunk and act
    like men.

—Anonymous

No means No, my brother.
Are you deaf in your ear,
motherfucker?

—Bitches With Problems
(song lyric from "No Means No")

Shopping

I was street-smart—but unfortu-
nately the street was Rodeo Drive.
                    —*Carrie Fisher*

The only thing worse than a
reformed cigarette smoker is an
early Christmas shopper.
                    —*Liz Scott*

I am partial to the grocery store
because it is one of the few places
on earth where I can afford to buy
pretty much any item I want. I
never find myself seduced by a
perfect melon, picturing my
friends seething with jealousy
when they get a gander at my
newest acquisition, only to look at
the tag and discover that it costs
$159 and needs to be dry cleaned.
                    —*Sarah Dunn*

The only time a woman has a true
orgasm is when she's shopping.
Every other time she's faking it.
                    —*Joan Rivers*

I would rather have a sharp stick
in my eye than go shopping.
—*Kate Clinton*

Buying something on sale is a very
special feeling. In fact, the less I
pay for something, the more it is
worth to me. I have a dress that I
paid so little for that I am afraid to
wear it. I could spill something on
it, and then how would I replace it
for that amount of money?
—*Rita Rudner*

Solitude

Laugh and the world laughs with
you. Fart and you sleep alone.

—*T-shirt slogan*

I'm single because I was born
that way.

—*Mae West*

I think, therefore I'm single.

—*Lizz Winstead*

One of the advantages of living
alone is that you don't have to
wake up in the arms of a loved one.

—*Marion Smith*

We're all in this together—by
ourselves.

—*Lily Tomlin*

Solo Sex

Sex is like bridge. If you have a
good hand, you don't need a
partner.
—*Anonymous*

At the girls school I attended they
have very strict rules: Lights out at
ten. Candles out at eleven.
—*Anonymous*

SELF SERVICE
There once was a woman named
    Doris.
Who spent her time with her
    clitoris.
She expertly knew
All the right things to do,
Saying, "Anyone else would just
    bore us."
—*Nina Silver*

I think Philip Roth is a great
writer. But I wouldn't want to
shake his hand.
—*Jacqueline Susann*

How lucky we are that we can
reach our genitals instead of that
spot on our back that itches.
—*Flash Rosenberg*

We got new advice as to what
motivated man to walk upright: to
free his hands for masturbation.
—*Jane Wagner*

THE POOR WOMAN'S VIBRATOR

The South

I'm going to write a book about
the South. I'm going to call it,
"When Beautiful Places Happen to
Bad People."

—*Brett Butler*

Sports

Boxing is like ballet, except that there's no music, no choreography, and the dancers hit each other.

—*T-shirt slogan*

Whoever said, "It's not whether you win or lose that counts," probably lost.

—*Martina Navratilova*

If you're playing against a friend who has big boobs, bring her to the net and make her hit backhand volleys. That's the hardest shot for the well-endowed.

—*Billie Jean King*

YOU TAKE A BAT
YOU TAKE A BALL YOU TAKE
A GLOVE & WHAT HAVE YOU GOT?

AMERICA'S FAVORITE PASSTIME... SHOPLIFTING.

Stress

I read this article. It said the typical symptoms of stress are eating too much, smoking too much, impulse buying and driving too fast. Are they kidding? This is my idea of a great day!

—*Monica Piper*

Texas

Texas, where men are men and women are mayors! The Great State, where the men rope cows and the women run the place!
—*Molly Ivins*

Television

The whole world isn't watching anymore—it's renting videos instead.

—*Julia Willis*

Television has proved that people will look at anything rather than each other.

—*Ann Landers*

I'm at a point where I want a man in my life—but not in my house! Just come in, attach the VCR, and get out.

—*Joy Behar*

My children refused to eat anything that hadn't danced on TV.

—*Erma Bombeck*

I eat too many TV dinners. I've gotten to the point where every time I see aluminum foil I start to salivate.

—*Ellen Orchid*

Therapy

The problem with therapy is it takes me more than 50 minutes to calm down enough to get in touch with my anxiety.

—*Lori Sprecher*

Freud is the father of psycho-analysis. It has no mother.

—*Germaine Greer*

I went to a conference for bulimics and anorexics…The bulimics ate the anorexics.

—*Monica Piper*

My therapist told me to use some imagination while making love with my husband. I said, "You mean imagine it's good?"

—*Anonymous*

I DONT EVEN HAVE THE COURAGE TO BUY IT,
LET ALONE HEAL.

Time

The future isn't what it used to be.
—*Linda Moakes*

Things just *seem* to get lost—
they're really waiting for you in
next week.
—*T-shirt slogan*

I've been on a calendar but never
on time.
—*Marilyn Monroe*

A seminar on time travel will be
held two weeks ago.
—*T-shirt slogan*

The day after tomorrow is the
third day of the rest of your life.
—*T-shirt slogan*

Truth

I never know how much of what I
say is true.

—*Bette Midler*

Twins

We were born 10 minutes apart,
Adrian first. She always said she
was the real baby, and I was a kind
of backup.

—*Adair Lara*

Underwear

My Playtex living bra died—of starvation!

—*Phyllis Diller*

Brevity is the soul of lingerie.

—*Dorothy Parker*

NIGHT OF THE LIVING BRA

I'll tell you what Victoria's Secret is. The secret is that nobody that's 34 inches or 34 years can fit into that shit.

—*Mary Ann Nichols*

A lady is one who never shows her underwear unintentionally.

—*Lillian Day*

Never Heave Your Bosom in a Front Hook Bra. (book title)

—*Liz Scott*

Like every good little feminist-in-training in the sixties, I burned my bra—and now it's the nineties and I realize Playtex had supported me better than any man I've ever known…

—*Susan Sweetzer*

Vegetarians

Vegetarians eat vegetables—I'm a humanitarian.

> —*T-shirt slogan*

Have you changed your tofu water today?

> —*T-shirt slogan*

I'M A VEGETARIAN NOT BECAUSE I LOVE ANIMALS BUT BECAUSE I HATE PLANTS

War

The battle of the Gulf was won on
the playing fields of Atari.

         —T-shirt slogan

If women ruled the world and we
all got massages, there would be
no war.

         —Carrie Snow

Before the Gulf War started, a
friend of mine proposed that Bush
and Hussein go off to a small room
together. I figured she'd say that the
two of them should just slug it out.
But no, she suggested that they go
into the room, close the door, pull
down their pants, and compare
penis sizes. Whoever's was bigger
would be declared the winner and
everybody could go home.

         —Ellen Orleans

Non-violence is a flop. The only
bigger flop is violence.

         —Joan Baez

Women

God made man, and then said I can do better than that and made woman.

—*Adela Rogers St. Johns*

We haven't come a long way, we've come a short way. If we hadn't come a short way, no one would be calling us baby.

—*Elizabeth Janeway*

Any woman who has a great deal to offer the world is in trouble. And if she's a black woman, she's in deep trouble.

—*Hazel Scott*

A woman without a man is like a fish without a bicycle.

—*Gloria Steinem*

The only problem with women is men.

—*Kathie Sarachild*

Work

Work is the price you pay for money.

—*Graffiti*

Adults are always asking little kids what they want to be when they grow up because they're looking for ideas.

—*Paula Poundstone*

An acceptable level of unemployment means that the government economist to whom it is acceptable still has a job.

—*Graffiti*

There are very few jobs that actually require a penis or vagina. All other jobs should be open to everybody.

—*Florynce Kennedy*

You can name your salary here—I call mine Zelda.

—*Graffiti*

The problem with trouble shooting is that trouble shoots back.

—*Anonymous*

I work to get away from my cat.
> —*Bumper sticker*

Ricky Ricardo: You think you
> know how tough my job is,
> but believe me, if you traded
> places with me, you'd be
> surprised.

Lucy: Believe me, if I traded
> places with you, *you'd* be
> surprised.
> > —*I Love Lucy*

I think of my boss as a father
figure. That really irritates her.
> —*Mary Jo Crowley*

Whatever women must do they
must do twice as well as men to be
thought half as good. Luckily, this
is not difficult.
> —*Charlotte Whitton*

Afterword

When I said up front that *Glibquips* wasn't a reference book—I lied!

Glibquips is the sixth book in the *Women's Glib* women's humor collection series, a set of books that explores the world of women's wit and humor in all of its manifestations. These books have been enjoyed by thousands of readers, studied in women's studies courses and purchased for many library collections. I'm happy that my books have helped further an appreciation for contemporary women's humor. (I'm even happier that I've helped expand the audience of the women whose work I publish.)

The first *Women's Glib* books focused on cartoons and written humor. Recently, at the suggestion of my publisher, I began to study women's spoken and performance humor as well. The resulting book, *Funny Business: The World of Women Comics*, will be published later this year.

In deciding which performers to include in *Funny Business*, one of the first places I turned was to quote books. Quote collections are a great way to discover whose words have made a difference. (They're one way a culture keeps track of itself, which is why they're so often found in a library's reference section.) I knew that the comic performers whose funny observations and one-liners turned up over and over in the many quote books I consulted would need to be included in *Funny Business*. However, a great deal of the material included in *Glibquips* can't be found in other quote books. In part this is because as a humor editor I have access to so much fresh material. But it's also because many editors shy away from humor they consider too "political" or "controversial." You'll find Phyllis Diller in most collections, for example, but you probably won't find Lea Delaria.

Why a collection of humorous quotes by women? (Besides the fact that it will make you laugh out loud?) Because mainstream culture tends to discount women's words, and because it also tends to discount humor. Wit isn't solemn, so it often isn't "taken seriously"—even wit that deals with important issues. One thing I've learned editing these books, however, is that comedy is communication. What women laugh about is what we care about. Over and over again, as I interview women comics, they tell me that their humor is based upon what's closest to their hearts. Often it's inspired by what "bugs" them. Over and over I'm told by women who are in the business of making us laugh that the best comedy always comes down to "telling the truth."

My goal with this book, as with all the books in the *Women's Glib* series, is to help women humorists tell these truths. Just as important, I want to help develop an audience for their work. If you find that a writer's wit appeals to you, look her up in the Resources Section. Get her books! If you find that a performer's wit appeals to you, follow and support her comedy career. Catch her act when she comes to town. Buy her tapes. Watch her on television. And "stay tuned"—you'll learn more about most of the women comics whose words you've enjoyed here in *Funny Business*.

Resources

Roseanne Arnold, Roseanne: My Life as a Gal; I Enjoy Being a Girl (audio); "Roseanne" (tv show).

Bertice Berry, "The Bertice Berry Show" (NBC talk show).

Erma Bombeck, *Motherhood: The Second Oldest Profession*; *Aunt Erma's Cope Book*; *At Wit's End*.

Rita Mae Brown, *Rubyfruit Jungle*; *Venus Envy*; *Six of One*; *Southern Discomfort*; *Sudden Death*; *High Hearts*; *Starting from Scratch*; *Bingo*.

Bret Butler, "Grace Under Fire" (ABC sitcom).

Jane Caminos, *That's MS Bulldyke to You, Charlie!* (Madwomen).

Kate Clinton, Live at the Great American Music Hall (audio); Babes in Joyland (audio).

Cathy Crimmins, *Curse of the Mommy*; *The Quotable Cat*; *The Official YAP Handbook*; *Entre Chic*; *The Secret World of Men*.

Ellen Degeneres, "These Friends of Mine" (sitcom).

Lea Deleria, Bulldyke In A China Shop (audio).

Rhonda Dicksion, *The Lesbian Survival Manual* (Naiad); *Stay Tooned* (Naiad).

Phyllis Diller, *The Joys of Aging and How to Avoid Them*.

Nora Dunn, *Nobody's Rib*.

Nora Ephron, *Heartburn*; *Crazy Salad*; *Wallflower at the Orgy*.

Carrie Fisher, *Surrender the Pink*; *Postcards from the Edge*.

Cynthia Heimel, *Get Your Tongue out of My Mouth, I'm Kissing You Goodbye!*; *If You Can't Live without Me, Why Aren't You Dead Yet?*; *Sex Tips for Girls*; *But Enough about You*; *A Girl's Guide to Chaos*.

Nicole Hollander, *Everything Here Is Mine: An Unhelpful Guide to Cat Behavior*; *Tales from the Planet Sylvia*; *The Whole Enchilada*; *You Can't Take It with You, So Eat It Now*.

Judy Horacek, *Life on the Edge*.

Molly Ivins, *Molly Ivins Can't Say That, Can She?*; *Nothin' but Good Times Ahead*.

Erica Jong, *Fear of Flying*.

Alice Kahn, *Multiple Sarcasm*; *My Life as a Gal*; *Luncheon at the Cafe Ridiculous*; *Fun with Dirk and Bree*.

Jean Kerr, *Please Don't Eat the Daisies*.

Florence King, *Reflections in a Jaundiced Eye*; *Confessions of a Failed Southern Lady*; *When Sisterhood Was in Flower*; *WASP, Where is Thy Sting*; *Southern Ladies and Gentlemen*; *He: An Irreverent Look at the American Male*; *With Charity Towards None*.

Kris Kovick, *The Thing I Love about Lesbian Politics Is Arguing with People I Agree with.*

Adair Lara, *Welcome to Earth, Mom!*

Fran Lebowitz, *Metropolitan Life*; *Social Studies.*

Patty Marx, *Now Everybody Really Hates Me* (children's book); *You Can Never Go Wrong by Lying*; *Blockbuster*; *How to Regain Your Virginity.*

Bette Midler, "A View from a Broad."

Dorothy Parker, *Enough Rope*; *After Such Pleasures*; *Death and Taxes*; *Lament for the Living*; *Sunset Gun.*

Stephanie Piro, *MEN! HA!* (Laugh Lines Press).

Karen Ripley, All Out Comedy (video).

Joan Rivers, *The Life and Hard Times of Heidi Abromowitz*; *Enter Talking*; *Still Talking.*

Rita Rudner, *Naked beneath My Clothes.*

Liz Scott, *Never Heave Your Bosom in a Front Hook Bra*; *Never Sleep with a Fat Man in July.*

Judith Sloan, The Whole K'Cufin' World (audio).

Lori Sprecher, *Anxiety Attack* (Violet Ink).

Gloria Steinem, *Outrageous Acts and Everyday Rebellions*; *Revolution From Within.*

Judy Tenuta, Buy This, Pigs! (audio); *The Power of Judyism.*

Lily Tomlin and **Jane Wagner**, *The Search for Signs of Intelligent Life in the Universe* (available both as a book and also as a video); Ernestine: Peak Performances (video); Lily For President (video); Lily Tomlin: Appearing Nitely (video); Lily: Sold Out! (video).

Venus Envy, I'll Be A Homo For Christmas (audio).

Julia Willis, *Who Wears the Tux?* (Banned Books); *We Oughta Be in Pictures* (Alamo Square).

Recommended Humor Magazines

Comic Relief, P.O. Box 6606, Eureka, CA 95502

The Funny Times, 3108 Scarborough, Cleveland Hts., Ohio 44118)

Girl Jock, 2060 Third Street, Berkeley, CA 94710

Hysteria, Box 8581 Brewster Station, Bridgeport, CT 06605

Laughter Prescription Newsletter, Box 7985, Northridge, CA 91327

Light Magazine, Box 7500, Chicago, IL 60680

About the Author

Roz Warren, a happily married radical feminist mom, is the editor of the ground-breaking *Women's Glib* humor collections.

A frequent speaker on women's humor, Roz has given the slide show she developed from cartoons in her books at many libraries, women's groups and bookstores. She writes about and reviews humor for *Feminist Bookstore News*, *Hysteria*, *The Laughter Prescription Newsletter* and *Sojourner Magazine*.

✳

The Crossing Press
publishes a full selection of humor books.
To receive a free catalog,
please call toll-free
800-777-1048